THE CONTINUATION

THE CONTINUATION

Norman Harris

To order additional copies of this book, contact:
Xlibris Corporation
1-888-795-4274
www.Xlibris.com
Orders@Xlibris.com
103783

CONTENTS

Greetings, Hope the reader of this document is in good spirits.

Not so sure of this existence anymore. Doesn't make sense. We the human beings devour each other like zombies in a horror movie. There must be another place where life grows as "One". To live through the flesh is death. Seems that real "Life" is beyond comprehension, above thought, non-linear, very beautiful. The flesh blocks the soul from seeing the truth so we die in darkness, forever wandering. We must escape the prison of the mind and flesh so that the light shines from within and the world may see the glory that is "Life". Only God can make this happen. Hope is all we have now.

Patience is what we need to realize Hope's potential. "How" is a word used in death not life. Faith is "Life's" word. ALL THINGS ARE POSSIBLE TO THOSE WHO BELIEVE.

THE GENESIS STORY

The condition of man can be readily understood by the study of the Genesis story. Man the likeness of God/Son of God. God cannot be seen hence man cannot be seen. So what man calls his life is really earth dust. The Lord God said to Adam "where are you?". Since God is real, and Adam was asked "where are you?" then it must be that Adam was no longer in "existence". Mankind questions God's existence but it is really mankind's existence that is in question. See Genesis 3-9 and Hebrews 4-13. We know God sees everything (Heb 4-13) so it cannot be that the Lord didn't see the dust of Adam. But the real part of Adam was no more. He was no longer in existence. All that was left was the dust which is the earth. So fear enters. Fear doesn't come by God. Fear is a component of death. Mankind fell from "God-like" to no more. What a fall it was! Fear is a component in the unknown. To fall from "God-likeness" is to produce great unknowns and great fears. Terror grips mankind like some devouring lion. The dust of man is the same dust of the earth that dinosaurs and other creatures before were of. There is nothing new under the sun. The same water, air etc. So man the dust is just the current state of the earth today. But the true man is no more. He died from God-likeness to no more. So mankind today functions as mere beast. Animals of sorts. Without the spirit of God we are nothing. The likeness was our Governor, our controller to keep us harmonized with nature and each other (1st John 1-7). Without the likeness we live like beast devouring each other through fears that aren't real. There are no good or evil persons on the earth. There are the living and the dead. The darkness keeps us from seeing each other as one. There is only one life on the earth not 6 billion. We are one. Our voice should be as one. Not by control or fear but life as one. We are one we cannot be seen, just like God. The physical bodies are merely parts of the earth that move. The bodies were formed to till the earth. It is understood.

THE TREE OF THE KNOWLEDGE OF GOOD AND EVIL

Throughout the readings it has been understood that God wants us to be "good". However, Genesis says that God didn't want us to eat from the tree of the knowledge of "Good and Evil". "Evil" was understood but why not "Good"? The whole premise of the Bible seemed to be about being "good". So we have a seeming contradiction why would God not want me to have knowledge of "good"? Seems that Good and Evil have the same effect on a life force, they create a perspective that isolates or separates one from the other. A subtle way to initiate separation in the "one" life. It seems as if you are gaining some wisdom but in fact it is driving a division between life forms. We war against each others on this principal. "I" am a good person so you must be evil, how else can "I" be good? If all is good there is no good. The "good" cannot be seen without the "evil". The true enemy is the knowledge that brings separation. The beautiful life dies when it contacts this tree. The light darkens because of "perspective". We no longer see life as "one" but we say "I" as though we have a life of our own. It is the nature of the dead. So Adam (our father) died. Mankind has since walked in darkness and most still do. In reality we cannot be seen, known or comprehended that is impossible. There is no "I". See Ephesians 5-8, Col 1-13, 1 Peter 2-9, 1 John 1-5.

VOICE

Lets discuss "voice" in Genesis. It is written that God said "Let there be light" and there was light. The voice of God is it sound? Mankind hears voice with his ears. Is God's voice ambient sound? Adam said I heard your voice "walking" in the garden. Does voice walk? When God said "Let there be light" who heard it? In a linear thought pattern the conclusion would be yes, it is ambient sound. But voice "walking" walking is not a metaphor that designates voice! Walking designates substance. God's voice "Is". When he speaks things exist have substance. When we look at existence we see and hear God's voice. The repetitious nature of the creation story when God repeatedly says "Let there be" and things are is neither ego or boasting(linear thought believes it is). Since no darkness is in God it cannot be ego. God is teaching us his voice through repetition. All of His son's will have the same voice. For example Adam(before the fall) was told that whatever he called creation that would be it's name. Only God's son would have such authority. God' son who's voice is God's voice. We speak in the one voice.

THE GARDEN

The garden is neither a place or time it is life. Through these formations of dust we call our lives we are responsible for its maintenance. Without the Governor this is impossible. Because man died and taken a linear and mathematical approach towards life he is not capable of sustaining it. All of his solutions have side effects. What solves one problem creates a thousand more. He is not capable of seeing that his fall is the condition not the particular problem before him. So he suffers. Mathematical equations are bound by error. They must by nature produce a solution at the end of the equation. Life never has a single answer. 1+1 could be 50 or 6 billion. Life designates the story. Man in his current state cannot designate life. He touches it and it dies. The formula man + knowledge equals God is a mathematical construct with a false answer. God is never equaled. In fact all was lost. Mankind is now stuck in the belief that the only things possible are those which he can compute. God would appear to man as foolishness. Man would have to humble himself and become childlike in order to believe and see the richness of God. Mankind often says certain things are impossible, but after another generation passes whose minds are not clouded by the old knowkedge, the impossible things of one generation become possible to another. History has shown that to be true. Clarity makes all things possible. Knowledge has a side effect it promotes some and hides many. Our cures have side effects because they are borne in knowledge. God's cure are perfect they are borne of clarity. In summary Man the son/Likeness of God died. The king of this world was exiled. The entire planet i.e. creation waits for the return of the sons of God so that the garden is sustained again. Without the Son's of God the earth will not give it's best. Mankind is surviving on the least by the sweat of his brow. In his original state all life flourishes. In his fallen state all life struggles. The resurrection of man is the primary objective. WITH GOD ALL THINGS ARE POSSIBLE.

THE CAIN AND ABLE STORY

The Cain and Able story is particularly interesting in that it established a template for giving. Able gave the first fruits(or best) that he had while Cain succumbed to the nature of "I" wherein he kept the best for himself and gave God what was left. This left him vulnerable to the darkness. So the Lord warned him that sin was at the door and it's desire was to have him. Yet the Lord told Cain" you must master it". Cain in his rage slays his brother to remove the comparison. The side effect of his solution is evident. In the good and evil environment mankind continues to make calculations (Rev 3-18). He is always wrong. Something is bound to go astray. He is surprised when the outcome is not as he calculated. What variable has affected his calculation? His solution should have worked. The Able example is one where Able humbles himself to the majesty of life and harmony reigns(God was pleased). Since God was pleased Able was in harmony. Calculations abrupt/stop the life forms from being in harmony with God/one. The evidence appears in the biology as a sinful act. To abrupt and stop harmony with God is death. By the time a sinful act is seen in reality it has long since invaded the soul. The rhino virus is the cause for a cold. Sneezing is a symptom. By the time you see the sneeze the virus has long established itself. Sin is the virus. So we use the law to treat the symptoms we use life to effect the cure.

NOAH'S ARK

A story of faith and holiness. Noah by all accounts would not be considered a "good" person by today's standards(he was passed out drunk). Perhaps he over indulged to some degree. But God chose him because of his "faith". It was his faith that made him righteous. God was disturbed to find that man had filled the earth with violence and death. This was the results of sin. To stop the flow of death God collects a remnant and destroys the rest. A sort of chemotherapy approach. In order to kill the cancer cells other cells die also. Mankind may not have survived this long without this. All this did was slow the progression of death. It was not a cure. But it provided time to effect one before man could destroy himself. We must remember that there were probably babies children etc. God destroyed them all. Aren't babies innocent? What about the children? Surely they could be salvaged? But God sees man as one. Noah was only saved by his faith(faith saves). This wholesale destruction of living beings was merely attacking the symptoms of sin. God hates sin. He tolerates it for so long then he must act. If all life is one sin has the potential to spread everywhere. This will not be permitted. Man seeks to protect his life. God seeks to protect all life. If a human had a cancer in his body he would seek to destroy that cancer to preserve his life. God seeks to destroy sin to preserve all life. Mankind sees himself as the crown of life while he is merely a component of. A loved component but a component nevertheless. So if we see God as the keeper of all life and man as a infected component this approach is understood.

ABRAHAM

From the lineage of Noah springs Abraham son of Terah. Lot(Abraham's nephew) was with Abraham because Terah and Lot's father had passed on. Through Abraham God makes his first promise of long term reconciliation of mankind. He says through Abraham all nations and peoples will be blessed. We cannot speak of Abraham without mentioning "Melchizidek". This is a priesthood so important but yet neglected in so many discussions of the redemptive process. His priesthood "is" the priesthood of the redemptive process. It is not: repeat not the Levitical priesthood wherein the law is established but after the order of Melchizidek is the redemptive process. Why is the redemptive process after the order of Melchizedek and not the Levitical priesthood? As will be further seen God establishes the Levitical priesthood first. But the jewel is really the order of Melchizedek and his priesthood. There is something unique regarding the order of Melchizedek but we cannot rush this process. So we will later in this discourse discuss the Levtical priesthood first so that we may appreciate the order of Melchizedek. Abraham went to war with the kings so that he could rescue Lot and his possessions for lot had been captured in a war with several kings. He was successful and upon his return met Melchizedek (king of Salem/king of peace). At that time Abraham paid tithes to Melchizedek and he brought out bread and blessed Abraham(Gen 14:19-20). This is very significant because it establishes a higher priesthood over the Levitical priesthood.

THE OTHER

There is no such thing called God and other. There is either God or the lie called "other". If God is all things than there can be no "other". "Other" is the lie upon which "I" is relied upon. God is real there is no "I". "I" says God does not exist. "I" must die to see God. If there is "I" there is no God. If there is God there is no "I". They are opposite or opposed. If you sense "I" God is dead to you or better stated you are dead to God. If you sense God there can be no "I". God is the light "I" is the darkness. If man could see God all pain and strife would disappear. But because he sees only "I" pain and destruction reign. He is in effect "blind". Racism is a symptom of this blindness. Because they say they see. Because of sight they have become blinded. If they did not live by sight they would see everything clearly. Man has an anti-spirit vs. God. Man is "I" God is all. We pray sometimes in the "I" contemplation and receive nothing for God does not hear such request. God hears us when we pray in the "one" voice. That voice is God's voice. He cannot deny himself. If we pray in the one voice we know that God hears us. White and Black people will never come together it is impossible because black and white are separate by description. But if there is no "I" all peoples can be one. Therefore "black' must die and "white" must die along with all other descriptors that separate. We meet at "love". All are welcomed. The understanding is clear ; we must return to the "all" sensation. Man currently has the "I" sensation. You simply have to look at the world to see it's destructive greedy results. Some would say there are "good" people in the world. But good people are just as vile as evil ones. Obviously this takes some explaining. So called "good" deeds if the life form is aware that the deed is "good" it is vile. If the life form performs the deed from its heart without awareness that it is "good" than that is real and genuine. And the life form will continue to do so without being prompted by a moral measure. Mothers loving their children is a factor of creation. She is not being "good" as some suppose but as she was created she "is". If she is not loving her children (barring other circumstances sick etc.) than she died in her soul and no moral proclivity or law will fix that. A man loving his son doesn't make him "good" he is merely functioning as created. If bees stop

16

pollinating flowers would they be "evil" bees or malfunctioning bees? To knowledge the deed even if it is profitable or so called "good" is vile. To love someone is a function of life not a "good "deed. We recognize the benefit. If it is from the heart without knowledge it is real. If it is knowledged it is vile. In this world people want to be praised/rewarded for what they are simply supposed to be. We are supposed to love one another as created. Those are not "good" deeds. The human life form suffers a malfunction, that malfunction is called "sin". The law was initiated to treat the symptoms but life is the cure. Innocence is the condition where man must return. We must in a sense surrender these lives and go back to where we originated. Mankind for all practical purposes has left home and gone to a far away land. He is lost without his governor. He cannot eat from the tree of the "knowledge of good and evil". The soul is a pristine life force it cannot be tampered with. It cannot have a blemish or a spot. Once that that pristine soul is damaged only God can effect its repair. The soul that sins shall die. Immediate separation from God. The study of Genesis and the entire collection of Writings called the bible discuss and illustrates the fall and redemption of mankind, principally his soul. There is no other condition that affects mankind more directly than being separated from God. The consciousness called "I" in mankind must surrender to God.

SIN

S in and its effect is a direct response to contact with the "tree of the knowledge good and evil". When a life form becomes sinful it is as if the eyes are opened; it immediately becomes self-aware. The next step it takes is to protect itself. It feels overwhelmed by the environment and sees everything outside of itself as a threat. It no longer functions as a part of all things. It uses all things as a means to its own survival. Communication with it is virtually impossible. It has developed a "perspective" a dark visual that allows it to see only itself. To reason with it is virtually impossible. In many cases it must be discarded. In an instant it becomes a devourer by nature. Destroying and devouring everything in its path until everything in the area is destroyed and then attempts to move to a new area where there is more to devour. Fear is its motivator. Love is far away. The earth itself is being eaten by mankind. When it is depleted he will attempt to find another to repeat the process. If he is unable he will perish forever. To save mankind and all life this cannot be permitted. So the genesis story serves as a sort of "diagnosis" to the condition of man and how he contracted such an exotic ailment. In sin each life form exists in a personal universe of its own. It is as if there are 6 billion separate and distinct lives. Each has his own God etc. They may have the same so-called religion and yet see God totally different. They see this as being acceptable. Each ones "God" told them that they are "good" and the other is "evil". And you must destroy the other. And of course "God" is with "You". God helps me destroy my brother. Not realizing sin has darkened his mind to fight against what is essentially himself. Christianity, Judaism and Islam have these divisions. The ability to bring separation has even permeated the very arena that was supposed to bring life together. What a mess!! So sin is not just an act it is a spiritual disease that permeates the soul to re-direct it from God to "I". Once the soul goes to "I" it exists in a self imposed prison and is not capable of recognizing its condition. The soul is for all practical purposes asleep. In a dream world which exist only of illusion and lies. So that the only thing a man sees are those in his own mind. We war against the phantoms that our mind shows us. We see enemies where none exist. Fighting our fellow man when our strength is standing as one. We create devices capable of destroying all life simply to save ourselves. We are destroyed from within not from outside. There is no outside enemy that can threaten mankind. He is threatened from within. When the soul dies you lose sensation and you see the flesh. You become self-aware. All you have is the flesh and it doesn't have long. It is vulnerable to disease, lust, etc. There is no inner control or governor/God. So an external "law" is applied to control the flesh. Mankind has his control in the form of "law" (which is external) the rest of creation does not. As time passes laws appear where there was no need before. Man becomes more beast-like as time passes. So laws are passed/initiated to control him. After so long it is reasonable to expect that the constraints will cease to hold and a flood of beast inspired activity should ensue. The "law" cannot hold forever. All societies suffer great catastrophes amongst wealthy and poor when this occurs. Societies will find themselves hard-pressed to jail every single violator though they will try. So eventually the "law" must be discarded for a more excellent way. There is a war that is fought in high places where the seat of darkness exists to free mankind. "We fight not against flesh and blood". There can be no war against flesh and blood. This is why we turn the other cheek and use a non-violent approach. It is not an attempt as some suppose to be a good person but an excellent strategy against the forces arrayed against us. We recognize that all life is one so we fight separation not flesh and blood. So that there is no misunderstanding "laws" are not error for while mankind has no governor "laws are the best option.

CONTROL

There is another problem with "laws" they institute a system of control. The problem with control is that it generally kills life. Life is a "soft" explosion. A "soft" explosion causes no destruction but delivers the essence of life in every direction. Control has a tendency to halt that process. It may be a principal reason why things held in captivity tend to die. Without the ability to proceed in every direction life is stopped. True freedom has no control! So there seems to be a problem and that problem is "chaos". How can chaos be prevented without control? The simplest understanding is that it cannot without God. But first control/chaos. It can be argued that control and chaos are essentially the same. Control exists because of chaos. So if control is there chaos is a seething bubbling force waiting to break out. Mankind has no solution to this dilemma. Eventually control will fail and chaos will reign. The only way to prevent chaos is to return to God. In God peace reigns without control. In God life flourishes because control does not abrupt it. So while the law institutes control it also institutes death because life is stopped.

FORCE

Force is a method used in the good and evil understanding. The "good" guy uses force to achieve his goals and the "evil" guy uses force to achieve his goals. In many cases they use the same force. Why is force needed? Force is used to make things as "I" see it for some good or some evil. We see force as necessary in our police military etc. to ensure a safe environment. A law breaker uses force to break the law and reach some goal. Since force is some form of control something must die in the process. So in the current world it is impossible to effect change without something being destroyed. Force can take many forms, a few are economic environmental physical etc. so that the threat of loss is real to the person or object being forced. In order to defeat force you cannot return force for force this only enhances the use of force. The object of the force must be removed. It is doubtless that those who use force will continue to do so. Force seeks resistance. Force gains strength in resistance. Submitting to force lessens its power. Some will seek to take advantage of this. However the users of force face a dilemma; they ensure that a greater or equal force will be arrayed against them. So by the measure of force you build the measure of force you face. Some understand this principal and participate in endless arms race trying to stay ahead of the annihilation curve. The results of which will destroy all. Mankind has built his own destruction! Who wins when all life is destroyed? Yet we cannot change this path toward utter annihilation. In the history of the earth the only species that had the capabilities to destroy itself and the world is mankind. Some might consider this to be an indicator of intellect perhaps it is an indicator of illness, why would life destroy itself except it were ill? We find being the object of force distasteful and yet we employ it when it suits our cause. To exist without influence or force is a function of life. Man does not have life so he uses one of the powers that death illustrates and that is force. He cannot comprehend accomplishing a goal without influence or force. How can he make things as he sees it without force? To love without influence, peace without influence to propagate life without influence is Gods providence. It would be foolishness to mankind. So peace and life reign in God or better said because God reigns life and peace flourish.

In some mythos Satan is pictured with a pitchfork. The pitchfork could be a symbol of force. To move or influence with a sharp object. Everyone feels violated when force is applied yet we know no other way to accomplish an immediate or sometimes long-term goal. As was said before when force is arrayed an equal and opposite force will arise to counter. As force is increased so is the counter. After so long both sides have attained enough force to destroy both sides. In the end force will destroy the user. It is written" He who lives by the sword shall die by the sword" and also "Not by power nor by might but by my spirit says the Lord of Host". God simply does not use force. His presence is all that is needed for peace and life to reign. Mankind in his present state is bewildered by such power. God's ways are not mankind ways.

MELCHIZEDEK

The Light beckons us but we must shed the old dead man and walk in the light and peace of God. The Old Testament is a history of mankind's struggle to master his existence. A few walk in faith but many failed. There is an obvious learning of his inability to master his existence. He has failed at every opportunity even when he has witnessed the awesome power of God. So even if God were to show miracle after miracle he still could not bring himself out of the mire in which he has entrenched himself. So is mankind permanently lost? Is he forever falling short of the glory which is God. Mankind finds himself in debt; a spiritual debt but a debt nevertheless. In the midst of life but not able to walk with it. He can continue to hide as it were in his illusions of good versus evil. Using others as evil to make himself good. Or could he face the truth that none are good and all fall short of the glory which is life/God. So we have the "law' merely a temporary solution. Mankind with a history of failure to keep the "law" God and life to measure up to. Melchizedek a priest of the most high God is unique because he had no mother or father beginning or end of days. The Levitical priesthood was one where the sons of Levi made sacrifice for the chosen people so that their relationship with God could be maintained. This like the law was a temporary solution. Under the Levitical priesthood a priest had to make sacrifice every time someone erred to God. Partially because something of value had to balance the error committed. The error had to be paid for. Also they had to remind the people that they had fallen short of the desired result. Because the priest were temporary(end of days) the sacrifice was temporary. The sons of Levi did nothing but this so the rest of the people paid tithes to the priest for their service to God and the people (see Mal 3-8). So like the law the Levitical priesthood was a temporary solution. The priesthood of Melchizedek is the priesthood of light. No origin no end of days. Mankind often searches for a beginning but man was created in the image of God. We have no origin. We have no beginning, no end eternal. If we are one we are eternal. Human beings celebrate a birthday and fear a death day. But every celebration takes them to that day they fear. But we celebrate God we have no origin. The beginning is the end. We cannot

23

be seen or measured. The physical body is a mere shell that we wear. To search for origin is to search for death. If there is life there is no origin. Mankind has found a place and hidden himself in it. What shall happen to me he says will "I" be no more? He believes he has origin so he sees his end. The fear of death is overwhelming. He will do whatever he can to avoid it. He does not realize he is already dead at origin. If a human being is questioned as to their whereabouts before he was here or after he is gone he will mostly not know. This is an honest though dark assessment. Everything is based on this existence so it becomes everything. Now they have origin. Life is stopped because they have origin. When there is no origin you see the beautiful life.

So we have a high priest who has no father(no origin) He is the likeness of God(no origin) he is eternal. This priest can make sacrifice for us forever. This is a much better cure for what ails mankind an eternal priesthood. So the old Levitical priesthood and its imperfect solution has passed away. The New Testament and new priesthood now reign. We no longer have to make the daily sacrifice. The eternal one has delivered it for us. Our debt is paid and our conscious cleared. We are borne of life now. We have no origin. Life has no origin. God would be in essence be distasteful to mankind. We would be total adversaries. Mankind loves the taste of good and evil we thrive on it. Communism and capitalism both consider themselves good and will put that good upon you with force if necessary. Good and evil is how we make origin. Without origin we feel as though we have nothing. But if we give up origin we actually get life back. So the Christ teaches us that to lose your life is to gain your life. Many people can't see pass the biological to see the life at spirit. We would not recognize God. The scripture says the darkness saw him and comprehended him not. God would be a complete unknown. We would have to leave origin to meet God. To know God is to not know the world. To know the world is to not know God. Without origin mankind would never see death. The biology would continue in the regeneration cycle but mankind would never see it. Death would have no sting; it would be as if you shed some skin. The power of death over mankind would be lost so force and control would be of no effect. Praise God! Peace begins to reign. No origin no fear no adversaries no war just life and love. No death to fear. Martin Luther King jr said he had a dream that Jews and Gentiles, Catholics and Protestants, black and white would sing together "free at last" thank God almighty we are "free at last". We would all come together as one it was our origin that kept us apart. He saw the beautiful life. For his witness he was slain like most prophets. In his current shell man hates God and kills his prophets. We have come to the beautiful day we must act now while the light yet shines. It should never occur to a human being to hate anything but darkness. We should not have to be told to love one another. The fact that we are speaks volumes of our condition. At creation all God said was be fruitful and multiply. Sounds like a great time. In darkness we no longer have the fundamental essence of life so we have to be told what to do. While the rest of creation "is" we "do". "Is" is permanent "do" is temporary so that you may "do" the best thing or not. "Is" is a guarantee of sorts. We know that God will provide because God "is" love. Love is not under control It does not single out who to love it loves all. So if you love specifically you don't have love you have an emotion that seeks that emotion in return. If you fail to receive it you stop your love ; that's darkness. Love looks for nothing in return and has no control. For God so loved the world that he gave his only begotten Son. When the Son of God spoke was it to do or was it "is"? The example is "Let there be light" and there was light. The Son of God must speak in the same voice. His words must be creation words. "Love your neighbor" is a creation statement it is an "is" not a "do". "Do" is effort is "is". So the words of Christ are the words of the Father and they are life. He is the creator so his words are! Mankind has failed to "do" for centuries. The Son of God didn't come to earth to say "do" good. He came bringing life; life "is" and "is" is permanent. So the burden of "doing" is lifted in Christ. He has fulfilled the law and removed the burden. We are free to go. Real believers heap no burden of "do" on others for we know we couldn't carry them ourselves. We shall be above the law without the law. God will place the law in our hearts so that we are better than the law. The heart is autonomous to some degree because while the brain moves the hand it does not regulate the "heart" by thought. If something is placed in the "heart" it functions as "one" in the life form. To "do" is not necessary. There will be no more outside control; no law! We are no longer under the law. There is no more control no more captivity. Free indeed! Who the Son sets free is free indeed. Our Governor/God is restored and we no longer live by outside control or the law.

THE SEED

Now this seed of light starts small and must be fed continuously. It is written" lovest thou me more than these feed my sheep". The seed grows on the word of God which is love. The journey is one of faith and endurance. The environment for the seed will undoubtedly be hostile. The growth is an entire lifetime. The sooner it is begun the better. Some of the servants of God will plant and others will water but God actually grows them. We need more laborers in the field the harvest is coming soon. Faith protects the seed from being stolen and helps it endure adverse conditions. Some conditions include care for the world, care for self and basic endurance through tough times. Some will face threat of this worldly existence for the world will wage war against them. We fight and run this race to secure the prize; eternal life. It is an endurance race. It is written "He that endures to the end shall be saved". The world will try to force them into self again by deception or force. When there is great fear look for deception it is there. When the tempter came to the Christ(after he had been in the wilderness forty days) he used fear of survival to convince the Christ to go to "origin" to save self. Adam was defeated in the first confrontation however the Christ used the word and the attempt to force to origin failed. If it was successful fear would have ensued and darkness. However the Christ retort was "Man does not live by bread alone" and again "thou shall not tempt the Lord thy God". Having overcome the flesh and temptation he proceeded on. When the soul dies the physical body tends to gorge itself on biological pleasures and "lust" develop. The soul having once been connected to God yearns for his presence. Life is all sensation, we are sensors. When the soul dies the only sensation we have left come thru the flesh. We over-indulge in fleshly activities because the soul needs the connection to God. There is no measure of physical indulgence that can compare. The soul is essentially starving so it becomes "hot" never quite satisfied with anything that it has: so it covets. It is trying to fill the space that only God can fill. God is the "water" for the soul. The Lord said "he who thirst can drink freely from the water of life". When the rich man died and Lazarus also the rich man soul wound up in hell. He called out to Abraham(who was in "Abraham's bosom") for just a drop of water to soothe his burning soul. God and Christ is that water. So here we stand today gorging ourselves on physical indulgences trying to find the satisfaction that comes from God alone. The "hot" sensation causes us to have a covetous nature: we covet. The law expressly says "thou shall not covet" but because the soul is "hot" we are covetous by nature. So God has given us a law he knows we cannot keep. The law however is supposed to awaken us to the fact that something is missing. In his present state man is covetous because of the nature of his soul. He considers it "natural" although he does not want his possessions coveted. We do to others what we do not want done to ourselves. The Christ said "do unto others as you would have them do unto you" with our present nature this would be difficult. So first his words must be creation words and second unless the nature is changed how can we? So the Christ teaches us that we must be born again. This is obviously not a biological process but a spiritual awakening. The dry "hot" covetous nature is changed to a new peaceful God centered nature. For man this is impossible. Mankind cannot affect to the resurrection of the soul. It is written "not by works lest any man should boast". There is no "good" that can be done to resurrect the soul. Only by faith in God is this possible. As God resurrected the Christ he shall also renew our once dead souls into the newness of life. We wonder what happens at the time the flesh dies not realizing we are already dead. As we become more flesh indulgent our behaviors begin to reflect it. When you see the abhorrent behaviors in the children the disease has reached its maximum potential and the end is near. To live through the flesh is death. The flesh becomes "saturated" with indulgences, it has limitations but the soul is limitless. We are trying to satisfy a limitless soul in a finite body. The problem is self evident. It is written "you cannot put new wine in the old bottle". To live according to the flesh is beneath man like" a pig wallowing in the mire". There is a certain cheapness about it: instant gratification and short term goals no patience. We must have everything now. The spiritual journey requires patience, long suffering and endurance. We are "tried in the fire". God will not give you more than you can handle. When the flesh is denied the spirit grows. You could take all the possessions in the world and still not feel satisfied. The soul needs God!

THE POWER OF FORGIVING

Most people see forgiving as doing some "good". As we have discussed knowledge of "good" is a function of death. So why is forgiving a function of life? If someone has been harmed forgiving saves primarily the person harmed. It reduces the tendency to "origin". If forgiveness is not used there is a tendency to protect "self" and thus "origin". Forgiving prevents this from occurring. Not forgiving can be a subtle trick to "origin" So the Christ teaches us to forgive seventy times seven. This has a added benefit it releases the person that needs forgiving from debt. If he feels in debt he may tend to "origin". If he is forgiven he no longer protects "self" and the life can remain beautiful. So we see that forgiving saves both parties; that is great power. Life does this to fight off the infection of sin. It is part of the sin immune system. The beautiful life becomes hard when it tends to self. When the shell is hard more is needed to soften it. Forgiving softens the heart, keeps the life soft and beautiful. When the life hardens it dies. It is no longer capable of growth it is stopped. The beautiful life dies and separates from God. It feels alone; terribly alone. The soul must be protected it is all we have. We don't have the flesh it will return to the earth than what will we have. God harvest souls; he planted them here and put them in an environment to grow and multiply. The environment has been contaminated. Without the contaminated environment it can be argued that forgiveness would not be necessary. While we exist in this environment we need a strong immune system. If we were in the kingdom we would not need the immune system because there would be no tendency to origin. There are no "good" people in heaven only the redeemed. In order to be seen as "good" "evil" must be present. Neither exist in heaven; only holiness exist in heaven. When a mosquito bites it is exercise time for the human immune system. This keeps it from becoming biologically "atrophic". The bumps and bruises we experience in life are exercises for our spiritual immune system. Every error does not mean death. There will be growing pains. Gods grace is sufficient. We die to the world a portion at a time a little every day. A wholesale transformation would not take. This is why the "journey" is so important. It has been said "what is the meaning of life"? Life is the meaning of life. Life makes life and death makes death. This may be a reason why it took mankind so long to make machines. He has finally gotten far away enough from life to do so. Death makes death which is why everything we make now destroys life. The arrogance of our minds has blinded us from the truth. Every gain in knowledge is a loss of sensation or feelings. We are getting smarter but our hearts are getting colder. Instead of feeling our brother he is calculated. Slavery never happens in life it could not be conceived. Slavery is a product of a dead soul. God wants to save the slave and the slave owner. To free both is a win-win scenario. In the win-lose scenario no one wants to stand in the lost position. We all want to win. But in the win-lose scenario there must be a loser. This prevents reconciliation. We would rather be a wrong winner than a righteous loser. So to forgive has great power. It places us in the win-win scenario so that the debtor and the debt-holder may be free allowing reconciliation. We have to be careful to forgive because the darkness is very opportunistic. Not forgiving places us outside the providence of God and makes us vulnerable to darkness. To see the opportunistic nature of darkness one simply needs to read Job. When God removes the hedge of protection from Job darkness moves in instantly. Darkness waits for opportunity and strikes like a serpent rendering its victims helpless with spiritual toxins. The soul can wither away and die. So forgiving is a protectant as well.

THE CHURCH

The church is the body of Christ. The church like our bodies is a delivery system for life. It is not a hierarchal organization as some believe with ranking members. However each member has a working part just as our body does. Our body is a whole so is the church. Christ is the head of the church. So in the body the arms, feet, legs, eyes have necessary functions to assist the whole. They are not ranking members. There is no hierarchy or separation. There has never been an ear standing alone alive; not for long anyway. All parts must be one with the body. Also, without the ear the body has no hearing. There is no particular person heading the church, we are all members and workers in the church for the body of Christ. An apostle is not a ranking member in the body; they have a function which is no more important than any other. They do not rule over Gods people but they serve. A teacher in the body is not a ranking member either, another very important function in the body. The scripture teaches us that "God has given more honor to those members that lack so that there is no schism in the body". So we know that a preacher is not the head of the church, he is just a member in the body and a servant. Preachers are not to lord over the children of God but serve them as the example of Christ proclaims" I came not to be served but to serve" and again "He that will be great among you will be a servant . . ." When Jesus went to wash the feet of a certain disciple that disciple wouldn't let him. The Lord replied "than you can have no part with me". We are all servants to God. There are no human beings at the head church of God. So to sit in the high places in a so-called house of worship is error. We walk amongst the people as one. We are not differentiated by where we sit but by how we love and serve. Which one of us did not receive our salvation from God that we can boast? We humbly serve. Love is our honor garment not fancy robes and titles. If any man makes himself out to be something he is nothing. Some will say does not the scripture say "first apostles than prophets etc." This is true however it is not a ranking order. It is however an order of attack. The apostles come first to break the yoke of darkness. The prophets come next to proclaim the word of God. Teachers are next to enlighten the word and missionaries and preachers to spread the word. What we have is a very potent attack system, If used properly very effective in destroying darkness.

A divided church would be the same as a divided body. The so-called church resembles a divided body, arm here leg there and an eye missing. Anyone part of such an organization can realize for themselves the failure of such things. Christ is not divided!!! There is no such thing as a name on the church of God. Christ is the head of the church and there is no discussion. The houses of separation that carry the name of God are not of God. This statement will obviously produce some animosity but it is said. If there is separation know that God is not there.

THE JOURNEY

The journey of life is tough. We must surrender the item we value the most; our lives. This is not a biological interpretation but a spiritual one. We have discussed how it came about. To possess a life is death. This understanding has confounded mankind for centuries. Mankind sees the surrendering of life as being totally physical. It is the consciousness "I" that must perish, the physical body stays in the regeneration. As the Christ teaches us "He who loses his life will gain his life" and "He who keeps his life will lose his life." Everything seeks to "exist". This information was told by an agent of darkness. The agent said that envy, lust, greed etc. want to exist and they make their existence by "pimping" you. It seemed odd that such wisdom would come from an agent of darkness but darkness has wisdom. That wisdom is not Gods wisdom but it is a type wisdom nevertheless. So it stands to reason that if there is nothing for darkness to exist upon it will perish. Once you can be seen you can be attacked i.e. fed upon. When we are in Christ our lives are hidden in God. Being hidden implies something seeks us. When we are a conscious "I" we can be seen thus devoured. The scripture teaches us that Satan prowls the earth like a roaring lion seeking whom he may devour. The darkness corrals us and seeks to feed upon us. However God nourishes us and protects us from the predator. Hence the Lord is referred as the "Good Shepard" who cares for the sheep.

THOUGHTS

When God created all things there was no "thought". This understanding would be alien to mankind. Mankind exists today according to his "thoughts". When we observe our world it consists of the thoughts we have generated. It can be argued that without the thoughts of man the world would be a beautiful place. We are being destroyed by or own thoughts. When God sent the flood to the earth He told Noah that the "thoughts of man were evil continually. What if God saw mankind destroying themselves with "thought". We cannot attain to life by "thought". Thought can be cold and calculating. If we live by the heart we love by nature. The Lord says "My ways are not your ways and my thoughts are not your thoughts". When we are spiritually dead our thoughts are toward destruction. This cannot be prevented. When we have "life" thought is unnecessary. God has made us perfect for "life" we only live. There should be no "thought" in this place. It was pure and holy it should remain as such. When God finished his creation he said it was "good" there was no commandment to "do". We simply were to be fruitful and multiply. Excessive thought is termed "worrying". This exacts a draining effect on the life form. Stresses begin to develop and the body begins to break down. When we are dead stress squeezes the remaining life out of us so that darkness can feed. The apostle Paul wrote "We must bring under subjection every vain imagination and thought". If we stay clear all things are possible. Our thoughts keep us from seeing each other. Once the mind is darkened a brother can stand right in front of his brother and not be seen. Again this is not a biological reference. Our own "thoughts" blind us. We must be born again.

THE KNOWLEDGE

How can "the knowledge" be explained? This could not simply be to know that a rose is red. The "knowledge" is of existence. There is no knowledge to existence. Mankind will not find it because there is none. The knowledge puffs up mankind making him believe that he is aware of or knows existence. Descartes is known for the saying "I think therefore I am". He believes he knows existence so he says "I". In the Garden of Eden Adam ate of the tree of the knowledge of good and evil and promptly became self-aware. So God asked him "who told you that you were naked?" When the knowledge came Adam thought he knew existence. He became afraid and overwhelmed by the immensity of life. Fear is a result of that transformation. Mankind fears what he does not know. God has never left mankind; mankind has left God. Mankind has gone to knowledge. The fear that comes with the knowledge will destroy all. The nature of all things is faith. All things in existence are by faith. The reason God asks us to walk by faith is because it is the nature of existence. It is no special thing that we do it is the norm for all things. Mankind uses knowledge to see existence and thereby destroys it. There is no knowledge to existence at all. When the knowledge comes death and fear come with it. To get the knowledge something must be examined. The arrogance of decision making upon life begins. So he examines the other life form at his leisure no matter the cost. A wealth of knowledge has been gained through tortures and experiments upon humans and animals alike. The results being considered "worth the cost" as long as "I" am not the subject. Our own lives are considered above the cost while we lay others at the alter of "worth the cost". Leaders in the world send others to die for their country while keeping those who are precious to them out of harms way. The sacrifice of my children is "worth the cost" whiles another's are to precious to part with.

THE DICHOTOMY

There is a strong occurrence that seems to be ; God and the "other". Since God is all things we have a problem who am "I"? My existence versus God each is all encompassing. My sensation is that of "me" and if "I" am lost all is lost. Since both cannot be all encompassing one must override the other. If there is God there can be no "I". If there is "I" God will not be seen. When we speak our voice should be one with God by the nature of all things. God cannot be far off. We are one with him. We should feel a oneness with God an intimate relationship where we are as one. The sense of separation between God and man should not be. When the Christ Gave his Life the word says "the veil of separation" was lifted between God and man. Mankind must be awakened to his real existence; one with almighty God.

THE SON OF GOD

Here is a term that has been interpreted poorly throughout history. Islam believes it is an affront to God to say he has a Son. Christianity sees the Son of God as human beings see their own sons. There are references to other "sons" in the bible. There is the "son of perdition", "son of a female dog" the more colloquial term being "son of a bitch" Are they physical sons? Did a man produce a son with a canine? Does perdition have a son? How was he created? The son seems to refer to the essence or likeness of an object. Son of perdition is the essence or likeness of perdition. Son of a bitch is the essence or likeness of a female dog. Son of God is the essence or likeness of God. He is Gods actual essence hence the phrase "My only begotten Son". God gave us his very essence to save our lives. In the kingdom of heaven this would be practically unbelievable. God has sacrificed everything to save us. We must not reject such a great salvation. Therefore there has to be a Son of God for he is the very essence of God. He is God. We are his reflection. We appear as he appears. This understanding can be difficult for some to grasp but faith can help. Without the Son of God there would be no creation no life. Everyone that is not in darkness knows this. The Christ said I and the Father are "one". God gave us the essence and the essence gave us His life. This is above comprehension and understanding we must have faith. Without faith it is impossible to please God. Perhaps now we may at least understand why. So God having gave us his life gave us love for God is love. We "are" love. Our whole existence is love.

STANDING IN THE PRESENCE

S tanding in the presence of God is beyond comprehension, knowledge or any understanding. The love is beyond all understanding along with the peace and humility. In the presence of God one never feels the God/man comparison. He does not make us feel inferior to him. He makes us feel equal with him. It is written that the "Christ did not feel it robbery to be equal with God". In separation we don't have that same equal sensation. Only when we exist as one do we really understand the intimacy of our relationship with him.

OTHER ISSUES

The more substantive issues in the "understanding" express themselves in the words of Christ. It is written "not to build our houses on sinking sand. Now as a matter of realizing this we try to make sure that we do not make foolish investments in time, money or relationships. For example those activities produce short term results that are soon washed away. Perhaps this understanding goes far deeper? Suppose it was a reference to this existence. The physical existence is slipping through our fingers like sand in an hour glass. We are unable to control the flow or pick its moments. Also in order to capitalize in the natural requires a physical existence. The domain of man is ruled by those in physical existence. Seems simple to say but no "body" no effect. So if the effects of man are required by his physical existence he simply does not have long to secure his intentions. We know not what day we shall no longer walk the face of the earth. But as a matter of relationship we know that the moments in the body pale to that without. By faith we build an everlasting existence not one based on a physical prowess which is temporary but a spiritual one which is eternal. Building our houses on sinking sand is a reference to putting everything into the physical existence while leaving the spirit bankrupt. Since we need to store more treasures in the everlasting it seems logical to build upon the spiritual existence. This physical existence means nothing without a body. Without the body we cannot participate in the realm. The vast riches of the spirit would make the physical existence seem unnoticeable. Perhaps some minor influences like sex and hunger may flash but for the most part it should be under subjection to the God like image of the spirit. So to build upon the physical existence is the proverbial sinking sand.

THE LIGHT

All problems fail at the "Light". Mankind now finds himself in a race against time. Trying to find the essential elements to existence before his time expires. He has believed the serpent. He believes there is a knowledge to existence. He must destroy existence to open it and get information. One problem; there is no knowledge to it. He will always find an infinite number of calculations and smaller and smaller particles to infinity. He will never locate the "Higgs" element because it does not exist. The creator has made all things through faith. All forms of knowledge coalesce into a false front. We learn forever but never come to the truth. If a base element could be found it could not be all encompassing, if it were we could not know it. Also there is the void which has to be able to hold the offspring of the base element. So we face the fact that we cannot know. We walk by faith not by sight.

VOICE

The voice cannot be explained in detail perhaps in understanding. The one voice speaks through all living beings. It is the same voice all the time. If we speak in the one voice it is heard in every corner of creation. We speak as one. When the illusion of the singularity is no more the voice will be all there is. The sensation called "I" is headed toward a catastrophic end. It is as we speak folding in upon itself in a vain attempt to stay in existence. We are not singular life forms. We are a function of all a life called man; but only a function. We have our existence within Almighty God. We must die to the "I" existence and awaken to our true existence. What if we really are the Sons of God the likeness of him who is the Creator. Would we be better as these singular life forms bound in a prison of dust which shall perish? Or should we take our rightful place as heirs of the kingdom of God? The choice seems clear. Seems a great deception has befallen mankind. He must now awaken. While the transition will be rough the journey must begin. We must put off the old man and his devices. As we stand today we function as a cancer in life. Once we were life forms functioning for the benefit of all life. Now like cancer those life elements which once were for the body now work exclusively for themselves. They are now redirecting resources and devouring nutrients to maintain themselves to the ultimate destruction of the body. This sounds a lot like mankind. Mankind went through a sort of chemotherapy when the bible speaks of the flood where God eradicates the cancerous mankind. Now he has provided a way for mankind to be healed of his affliction. To turn his once cancerous behavior and existence back to a function of all life. We must be born again. All of creation suffers under the oppressive nature of mankind. The animals in the north, in the sea also in warm climates losing their habitations because mankind sees himself as an all encompassing "I". It is when we see that the life is almost expired that something says to some of us "stop!" We consume everything in our path and then realize that this continued behavior may spell the end to all life here on earth. Yet we have not come to the understanding that it is our very nature or natural for us to be destructive. Life does not consume it self unto destruction. Our species is dead from within. We have joined the Destroyer in consuming life, it must be stopped there is no greater issue in life. If we felt a oneness with life would we pollute the very water that sustains us? It is as though we are poisoning ourselves when we poison our environment. We live today in a toxic soup. We throw things in the earth to hide them from our presence only to see the results of this behavior in the not to distant future. Our children are born in a world of chemicals and false fronts; put in a artificial world and we wonder why they cannot feel. We nurture knowledge but the soul, heart and spirit are left bankrupt. Our children's hearts have become so cold life means nothing to them. They calculate every thing and feel nothing. Children used to be the holders of innocence but this world we live in has made their hearts run cold. Soon there will be no natural vanguards to life, no respect for the very existence each one of us cherishes so deeply. When we see pain and destruction happening to our neighbor we must not ignore it. If we stop it at our neighbor it may never come to our home. If we close our eyes to our brother's problems we may soon find ourselves in a similar dilemma. Am I my brother's keeper? Life is the centerpiece of all things. We sometimes believe that the things in the world make us happy. However if we had all the possessions in the world and no one to talk to or engage those things would turn to nothing in our eyes in 72 hours. Three days is all that is needed to realize that it is not good for man to be alone. We need each other it is the true nature of life. No one is expendable. Every life is cherished. "Love your neighbor as you love yourselves". Possessions only enhance us if there is someone there to recognize we have them. They are "dependent" upon there being someone who either has similar or lesser and the life form receives the illusion of acknowledgement. It is an illusion because no one is an amalgamation of his possessions. Although in this world we do act as though they were. No matter your possessions we still eat, sleep, die and awaken alike with little or much. Your possessions do not mean that you will grow wings or that your opinion is greater than another. Again in this world the rich are heard the poor ignored; this is largely an illusion. Sometimes you don't have to be right you just have to be rich. Few people ever listen to a poor man. Perhaps this is why the Lord came without monetary surroundings; only those who are pure of heart would hear. Judas in his betrayal sought only profit when he sold the Lord for money. The love of money is the root of all evil. So that we are clear there should be no bias against the wealthy. But those that are wealthy will find themselves in a struggle to stay grounded in humility. LET NO MAN MAKE HIMSELF GREAT IN YOUR EYES! Whether they have a little or much all life is one. There is no "super" man. It is written that the Lord asked a man "How do you see men" he replied "I see men as trees walking". The lord touched his eyes and said "how do you see men now" he replied "I see men as they are"

FEAR

Fear is not an original component of mankind. For lack of a better comparison it is as if our original programming has been overwritten by a viral program. We cannot and do not respond in the manner of our original designation. Fear is a motivator but it is a dark motivator. Fear hides subversive and malicious intentions. Fear and deception run together. When an entity uses fear it is generally trying to gain time and opportunity to install a lethal objective something it knows we generally would find abhorrent. Fear diverts our attention. We are so consumed by it we cannot see otherwise. Fear paralyzes life. A simple example is a beehive whose function is one of life in all aspects. If approached some of the bees will give their life to fend off an attacker without taking thought for their own existence. If fear could be introduced an attacker could subvert the bees from their original designation and steal kill and destroy the hives existence. The bees would no longer be able to sacrifice their lives for fear would paralyze their actions. Such an event has befallen mankind. Mankind in his original state would sacrifice himself to save life. How do we understand this? We know that it is the nature of God to sacrifice himself for man and man was made in the express image of God. The apostle Peter was told by the Lord "before the cock crows twice he would deny him three times". When Peter saw the persecution of life fear gripped him and he denied the Lord. The Lord knew Peter did not have the capabilities to stand so he told him what would happen. Man without God is extremely fearful to the point where he would deny God himself if his life was in jeopardy. The darkness knows this and uses it against us on a daily basis. We will not come to the aid of each other for fear of our own safety; closing our eyes to obvious situations to save ourselves. No one is immune. Whole nations destroy each other for self preservation. Each one of us would destroy each other for self preservation. This is the nature of darkness. When the Lord told Peter he would do this he said like most of us "I would never do that". We send soldiers to die for us and sit at home in fear. For his courage to mean anything we must show courage at home. A fearful nation will soon perish. Without the spirit of God mankind will destroy all to save himself. Once Peter received the holy spirit he had enough courage to "drink from the same cup" as the Lord which meant that he would suffer a similar death. The Holy Spirit gives us strength to suffer and ultimately not cherish our own lives unto death for the glory of God. Among those who will not inherit the kingdom are the fearful. So that we are clear it is not the strength of a man it is the power of God. It is written "God has not given us a spirit of fear but of power love and a sound mind". Mankind has no strength of its own we are wholly dependent upon God the Father. Every breath every movement spiritual or natural we are strong through God alone. Of ourselves we are nothing. If we are weak God is strong. If any man says he is something he is a liar. All who understand truth realize God is our strength. WORSHIP NO MAN! Martin Luther King should be honored for yielding to God. He himself was inherently weak. God was strong in him. We celebrate God not the vessel. This is truth not doing "good" it is merely the truth. Recognizing the truth prevents us from following the lie. No man can make himself great in our eyes. The error of Jonestown and others will find itself difficult to repeat if we remain at truth. Only God is great he alone is worthy of praise. All the Sons of god will make sure this is said.

THE PAIN

The pain in and of itself is a difficult understanding. We all suffer "the pain"; we live in it daily. We indulge in consumption to quell or quench it. When the body dies we can suffer with it. It is inflicted by choice. The sad part is no one has to feel the pain. Of course if you receive some bodily injury or some loved one is hurt or troubled we see this as pain. Those are temporary pains that will heal or time will sooth. The "pain" is everlasting. In it you find suspicions, jealousies, fear, restlessness and stress. All of these are symptoms of but not all inclusive traits of the pain. Some of us have lived with it for so long we have forgotten we are in it. We all exist today in an agony. Hard to believe, but there is a level of peace and tranquility we are born at that no longer exist in our awareness. We have come to accept the pain as normal life. In the destruction we simply say "that's just the how things are". Little children cannot fathom the behavior of adults; however by the time they reach adult age they have become part of it. Children of all races can play together adults cannot! If we could walk away from the "pain" we could come together just like the children. A spiritual being is in a "quiet agony" at "self" he is suffering the "pain". When we live at self we exist in spiritual agony. At the end of the physical existence the terror comes, we are spiritually bankrupt and squandered a lifetime not being aware of it. So the Christ took on the "pain" to himself in order to release us from the consequences. When we are born again we die to self releasing us from the pain. He who has an ear let him hear. We will be free at last. So there is technically no reason for any to suffer the "pain". We can do all things when we are in Christ. Physical suffering should not hinder a servant of God. Self is the only pain we avoid. We understand that absence of body does not stop the "pain", which is why suicide is meaningless; you still end up with the same agony. We understand that when we are born again in the kingdom there will be no more pain or suffering. Jesus said "let it be on earth as it is in heaven" Even though we have physical pain we have eternal peace beyond understanding. We cannot wait until the physical body is exhausted before we exit the "pain". We must act now while we have the time. God has been warning us that we can suffer everlasting pain because of the condition. It has been told that God sends people to eternal suffering but in truth we who suffer such a fate chose it. We do that simply by choosing "self" or "I". Conscious "I" or self is a crushing debilitating event to the soul. We must escape from this eternal trap. So to conclude the matter a spiritual being is in agony at "self". They cannot be fully aware of it while they are in the flesh.

NEED

This sensation is arguably the most difficult to overcome. Since we have basic needs like food, shelter, sex and so on it can be argued that needs are simply a part of life. But there are natural needs that come as being alive and there are added "needs". We all have basic needs as a function of existence. Those basic needs are obtainable by some measure of life. However it is mostly the added needs where we find ourselves vulnerable. The man who is least vulnerable to his needs will most likely succeed. Some added needs are of a technological, social, and financial nature. These sort of added needs serve to bridal the human spirit. We in effect become "thirsty" for things introduced into society as convenience which is then developed into a "need" These needs make us vulnerable to behaviors we would otherwise not be subject. We take advantage of each other if we find another in a state of need. Some of these needs could be considered to be a sort of "soft" addiction. "Soft" because society does not see the need of such items to be harmful but collectively all these added needs can deceptively convince us that we are deprived of something. Cell phones used to be a luxury now they have become a "need". If you want to buy a car and the seller surmises that you are in need he will use the occasion to exact a more than usual cost, needs make us vulnerable to "more than usual cost". In relationships if the other party detects there is a "need" they can and will most likely exploit this tendency to exact a more than usual cost. We weaken our resolve and in effect "put the hook" in our own mouth when we display need. The bait of our "need" snares us. An inverse relationship finds itself at work in our world; those who need get less those that don't need have things given to them in abundance. We must not show ourselves needy. By doing so we avoid "usury". Usury is exacted upon the needy. He pays the "more than usual cost". We must stay debt free in all aspects.

SUPER SIMPLICITY

S uper simplicity is as it sounds. There is literally no need for "thought". It is understood that there was a first man. He had no instructions, no laws, and no thought. He was the created the "Son of God". A term not merely suggesting lineage but mostly operational. In this place man was the likeness of God. Everything was cared for by man. So man is the engine so to speak of this place. If man fails this place will fail. As he was he was perfect. He was not required to figure anything out hence "super simplicity". Who told the first man how to have sex or love children? If he had no teacher he must have these things as a matter of creation. God has made things super simple. It confounds the wise who seek knowledge when there is none. The serpent deceives the first man with God-like knowledge. When God created man he said it was good that means nothing else was needed. He did not create man so that man could improve himself by knowledge. Only the Creator can make improvements to man. He cannot repair himself. There are no corrective measures. He must be born again. He will exhaust himself searching for a remedy. We must become as little children; not a reference to immaturity but one of being "super simple". The more knowledge we obtain the darker our hearts become. Thought stops the natural flow of love that instructs and guides us so that you literally have no need for anyone to teach you anything. We must learn who we are so that we may stand in the operational position as the Sons of God in this place. The earth and creatures are waiting for the emergence of the "Sons of God". When man is dead the earth suffers. When he exist as he was created the garden grows. So a marvelous thing happens; God gives us his life because we lost our own. THE MOST BEAUTIFUL STORY EVER TOLD. Even the solution to the dilemma is super simple. Just accept the gift of "LIFE" from God the Father through his likeness the Christ.

We may someday see the final clarity that speaks so brilliantly everyday had we taken the time to hear it. If only we weren't so busy with the day to day struggles if for one second we could forget of ourselves and open our eyes the dread of existence (that is to say death) would be a thing of the past. We seek to understand through "I' which only darkens the clarity. As we search the universe for new life we disregard the very essence of life we have before us. Who is to say that we would be the seed of the universe. So that we are clear no type of dialogue can communicate the gospel. He who has an ear will hear.

STIMULUS AND RESPONSE

Understanding Stimulus/Response is simple. We currently exist in a stimulus/ response environment. We react to stimulus by virtue of the physical nature we have become immersed in. We are moved by fear, greed, human love, and human happiness. Rarely will you see someone moving when they cannot protect or enhance self. Our lives now are a series of stimuli and response. There are entities natural and spiritual who understand this. They use this knowledge to move the masses at their leisure. But surely this would become boring after the user became proficient with it. So we may assume that it would lead to greater and greater attempts to stimulate. This gives the knower a since of "power". I can make this item do this or that if I stimulate this molecule or that DNA strand. It is why we make pigs green; to show we had the power to do so. Our television is a stimulus/response medium. We are bombarded daily with messages that seek to stimulate us to move in a certain direction. The messages are so exacting that even the colors and other subtle nuances are calculated. We are being led by our sensations, a sort of slavery. We are fed the images they desire us to worship. We hate the enemies they tell us to hate. We are willing to believe anything if the stimulus is strong enough. They study rats in a maze but they seek to apply the most lethal stimulus to humans. The criminal and cop uses stimulus to move the subject. The Germans were documented (as I am sure all have done this) as been very interested in understanding how human bodies reacted to certain adverse stimuli. So now that we understand the stimulus/response slavery environment what is the purpose? Since stimulus/response appears to be a force of nature why humans are slaves to its effect? The answer seems clear. Mankind must exist outside of the stimulus/response arena. If we were driven simply by instinct we would fit in stimulus/response. However we are not instinct driven we are outside of beastly realms. We are spiritual beings we cannot eat of this world. If we do we become entrapped in the stimulus/response realm. Then watch the human being use his intelligence to feed or satisfy stimuli. He can make devices without end because he is a spiritual being. If he were merely a beast he could not go beyond his creation. Because he is beyond mere creation nothing can be beyond him. It is why God confused his tongue in the story of the tower of Babel. As we trace the roots of stimulus/response it can be argued that it began at the Garden. Adam our Father was above stimulus/response then through his indulgencies of the creation he put us in the stimulus response realm. Immediately he felt fear, moved by the nature of existing. So we were born into this world of stimulus response. We retained some spiritual traits but in time they begin to fade as we put horror upon horror on one another. In our true nature it would never enter our existence to harm another (There is no law). Now we are mostly beast. We respond to all stimuli. We cannot resist. We are easily led astray by our own desire. Everything is for sale to satisfy the stimulus. We sale even our children to satisfy the area stimulated. To live by stimulus is slavery. So we say who has not given themselves to stimulus? Who has not eaten of that tree? There is such a One and he was the Christ. He was also tested to see if he would yield to the realm. After being led into the wilderness and bringing his flesh to exhaustion he was tempted to see if he would like Adam yield to sin/the realm. But the Christ refused to yield to sin/realm and did not respond to stimulus. When he said turn the other cheek he was teaching the nature of life that we should not yield to stimulus. But be ye Holy for I AM Holy. The entire message is one of restraint so that the power is not given to the adversary. So we must die to this world (aka the realm). There will be temptations but if we walk straight they will fall away as nothing. To walk crooked is to walk according to stimulus. Now again what exactly is the purpose of getting mankind in the realm of stimulus response? If man is reduced to this level he is obviously of no value for he is a slave, cannon fodder, to be used at the behest of the user. Mankind is being used. In Gods arms we grow and are loved, in sin we multiply and do not grow. Now back to the purpose, stimulus/response is designed to isolate or separate. Again it is a sense of power. If the proper stimulus can be applied we can separate out a certain element. Most of us are of certain physical indulgencies we are drawn in by our own lust. Once you are isolated you can be destroyed or used or pushed around. We have not power of ourselves. Natural hunters try to isolate prey. We are being hunted. The purpose of this hunt is to spread isolation in the nature of life. It is a vile disease that would destroy all that is life so that "I" might rule over all. The world itself is headed toward such an event, it has remade mankind in its image after its likeness and is called the god of this world. This is it's template of existence. This horrible existence is what it intends to replace the kingdom of God with. WE shall destroy this vile creation at its root. Its attempt to infect God with this diabolical evil will not go un rewarded. So to all that is mankind if you are capable of hearing this message take heed that you endeavor to walk straight. The devil seeks to sift us as wheat so that he may devour us. The nature of Life is "ONE" there is no I. Stimulus/response seeks to separate to isolate and bring separation in all that is ONE so that I may rule over all. Yield not to temptation it's a trap. Young African men do not yet understand this is how they are being manipulated. They often find themselves at the mercy of those who use stimulus to motivate. They kill life for shiny rims and gold chains, all of which fit into an S/R environment. Those things would lose their value if they did not respond so readily to them. No man can free another he is a slave in his own mind yet he won't free himself. We have the power to be free if we live above S/R. Do not allow your children to fall in love with the things, it can make them slaves. The devil will see them and devise a trap. If you show them Christ or the way to live a life free of S/R they will avoid many of the snares of the devil. We have a chance at a new beginning in Christ because he is free we are free. Free at last Free at last thank God almighty Free at last. If we look at the example of Christ in the storm; his companions were full of panic while the Christ was asleep. He asked them why they were so fearful. Their response was we are about to perish; they were responding to stimulus. The Christ removed the stimulus so that they no longer feared for their life. The Christ knew that they were yet part of the S/R environment even though they were his disciples. Peter (who the Lord said upon this rock I will build my church) tried to say that no matter what happens he would not deny the Lord. But the Christ understood that he was still part of the S/R environment and said to him that he would deny Him when he was stimulated the right way. He did not have the capability until the Christ gave him of his life. We must eat the bread of life. When he became born again his whole life changed from that of an S/R slave to a free man. This is the promise of God. The Christ could have never gone to Calvary if he was in an S/R environment; he would have saved himself. Had he fallen for temptation he could not be an example or sacrifice for us for he too would have been subject to the S/R environment. If we die to S/R we would actually live again. If we live in S/R we will die. That death is the real death. Those bodies belong to the earth in cycle. We were made in the image of God. Since God created all things it is not fit that he should be subject to his own creation. We are his sons and daughters we are not subject to the creation either unless we make ourselves slaves to it. Mankind must once again stand above creation; the position he held before the fall. We should be the rulers of this world not subject to S/R as we have become. The reason the term goy (cattle) is used is because we have yet to see that we are being herded and slaughtered. There is no excuse for the existence of WMD's except that some stimulus has pushed man in a direction to create his own destruction. Beware of those selling fear. All life is one there is no life adversary. If any of us suffers we all suffer. Arise from your slumber man and live. It sounds foolish to say that God would be subject to money or anything in this minor creation. So it stands to reason that mankind would see the foolishness of being subject to stimuli. Some know the Path and take it; some choose pleasure over God to there ultimate dismay. We should be one with God. We should be equal with God for it is God himself who said let us make man after our image our own likeness. God is a spirit. The Christ said I would that you would be one with God as I am; and again it is written that the Christ did not think it robbery to be Equal with God. There is a One who sat at the throne with God and saw that God does make man to feel inferior to him but holds him as an equal. We have reduced ourselves. The sense of separation between God and man is a result of creation indulgencies. The creation is subject to God in inferiority (because it is corruptible) and to man naturally; however we have stooped to the level of beast by wallowing in this flesh. Walk in the spirit and you will not be subjects. Those that hate life will induce stimulus to force a response; watch and pray. It is admittedly a difficult journey; it is very easy to live according to indulgencies. Why fight it? We see now that it is a path to destruction of the soul. A brief existence of pleasure for eternal agony; if it is understood there is really no choice. We may take the easy road or will we have faith and walk the Path. The reward for endurance is an eternal life. An amazing transformation takes place when we leave S/R; the love we exhibit is no longer affected by situation and circumstances. We are no longer slaves to the winds of S/R. We can do whatever task is before us without diversion because some entity can manipulate us to do its bidding. To give of ones self to the point of exhaustion of this earthly existence will be of some discomfort but it should not prevent us from doing that which favors life. There once was the understanding eye for an eye; now we do not return eye for eye because it is the nature of weakness. We return love for evil because we are not ruled by S/R. God could adjust every situation so that it wouldn't make us fearful but he has chosen a greater solution; He has made us impervious to S/R. Now no matter the situation we should not fear. This is not because we don't feel pain but because our resolve is outside the realm of such events. We will suffer but we will not yield. Remember the story of Job how the devil used all manner of stimuli against his life to prove to God that he would yield; yet he held his position. God rewarded Job for his patience and endurance. Each time the stimulus didn't give the desired reaction the devil requested from God to raise the level of stimulus. God allows this to the exhaustion of flesh but gave no room for the devil to attack his soul. All of the examples of the Sons of God are of this particular battlefield. They are tried to exhaustion then exalted. This exaltation is to exhibit to those who are still in chains the power and glory of God. If we resist the tempter we shall be glorified. We are all trained to respond to stimuli from birth. We should have been grown in an environment free from influences. This world should be clear no Good or Evil. It is written not to eat of the tree of the knowledge of Good and Evil perhaps now the understanding is clearer. Where there is Good vs. Evil there is death. It is easily seen if we die. But if we live at "I" we live in darkness; forever wandering and searching unable to see God anymore. What we now see is called "I" we live in this until the flesh is exhausted and the soul is lost outside God. "I" is a separate and distinct world from God; God does not live in "I" and "I" does not live in God. In our present state we could not join God; our natures would be entirely opposite. God is the same today yesterday and forever there is nothing that moves God; he moves all. He cannot be subject to his own creation. Mankind however is moved by every stimulus package that comes his way. If man could meet God he couldn't comprehend him. Man is addicted to stimulus; God is so far away from stimulus it is shameful to speak it. The addiction is clear we need more and more stimulation everyday because we are dead. We seek stimulus anyway we can get it. Like a dope addicted life form we need higher and higher doses. You don't recognize you are destroying yourself until you have died. The scripture tells us that men will be "lovers of pleasures more than lovers of God" Being addicted to stimulus is why people do what they do. The problem is that without that body you cannot be stimulated. If you die addicted to stimulus how will you get your fix? The spiritual agony must be tremendous; a being made in the image of God suffering an eternal addiction with no way of quenching that thirst. When is the last time we meditated in a peaceful place; a place free from influences and stimulation. Would we make better choices? Would our souls flourish so that the flesh would not be the dominant decision maker? It is certain that a clear head makes better decisions. Wisdom is found in those who recognize that all considerations have to be made above personal influences. This allows us to protect life whether it favors us or not. If we do what favors us only we have yielded to influence and brought corruption to our situation. God does not show partiality; if we exhibit this trait we are not the Sons of God. He has no respect of persons. If you love only your own this is not the love of God. Because we are outside of S/R our love touches all as it touches ourselves. There is no control.

EMERGENCE

Now we see that the new beginning has no influence. We are in a sense unable to see ourselves. So we walk by faith and not by sight. Since all of life is a series of emergence (i.e. we came from other life) who is to say that the end of emergence is mankind. Suppose a new life forms has its roots in mankind; do we have the right to prevent emergence? Do we have the right to abrupt the next species in the chain or ladder of life? Mankind has declared himself the end of all things. He is neither the beginning nor the end. The Christ said he is Alpha and Omega the beginning and the end. Emergence may be a continual process of which mankind may be just a speck in. There may be many houses that build the great house of life all of which emerge until forever never ceasing. **No life form has the right to stop this process. Those that do so bring death to all that is life.** We like all other life must come and go as designated for the glory of all life. The example is Christ gave his life. It is the process of giving that is tantamount to life. We cannot initiate a "STOP" in life. The new life must emerge there is no higher priority. At the highest level it is not about mankind proper; it is about the life force forever. No one is above that no one. Life does not stop it is everlasting. There has been an attempt by some life forms to stop life at their emergence. All life has given up its emergence to the continuation. Fathers give to sons and so on. Christ is the corner stone of the church the building blocks of a great life form. Had he not given his life he could not have emerged as he did in his new form. It is the way to glory. So the giving up of existence continues. But we may give birth to a greater life form who may give again until forever. If this is the case it is understood why God cherishes life so jealously. Who would want to stop such a marvelous event? It is here where we see the greatest distinction between God and the devil. God wants life continued, the devil wants what mankind wants; to abrupt life at its emergence. When a believer begins his journey it will probably begin in a church environment. They will wrestle with moral imperatives to seek a balance in this existence. Some will succumb to religious traditions and some will leave. Yet there will be some who seek the higher understandings and seek the Kingdom of God. The Kingdom is not morality it is the power of God to salvation. Seek and you shall find knock and the door shall be opened. It is unlikely that a large number of people will be able to hear this message. Only God can show them the light. The words used here are at best insufficient to say all that is required. Godspeed.

THE END OF DEATH

Death exists in the illusion that the emergence is stopped. To be trapped in the illusion means certain death. In life there is no death. Some will say that people live and die but that is merely a regeneration cycle life is not stopped. The real death is when life precedes no further, stops growing. Death holds its victim in a grip that seems unbreakable. Our souls are wholly dependent on being without limit. Death imposes an artificial limit on the soul to capture it in a confined space. We become singularly self contained. A reason why we act selfishly is because we exist as singularities in an illusion. We can't see anything else. We live in a saturated life environment and seek to destroy it. The whole cause of sin is to isolate. Without our ability to reach infinitely we confine or isolate and that is death to a limitless life. Fear is generated in the enclosure; we have been captured. If you are reading this and you know fear you are in a death grip from which you have not yet awakened. The Sons of God know not fear. (Witness the Christ) If he were of fear his all would have been himself and that is what he would save. The process of life "IS" there is no effort. We do according to what we are. If we are limitless we can love all. If we are dead we love only that self contained environment in our own illusion. No one can be more than what they are. Hence it is impossible for there to be a Good man. He will be as his soul dictates. If he is confined he will be selfish if he is free his love will be without limit. We have a victory over death. The Christ has defeated death so that no one has to suffer the stifling confinement of such an event. Although these bodies remain in the generation we never have to see death. All of the confining entities have been defeated. True freedom now is available to those who believe. There is no ability to confine in God; death is impossible. We shall be free of all influence and confining capabilities. The soul is limitless again and death (the confiner) is impossible. This does not require money, wealth or any other capability just faith. A true believer will never see death. So we have a visual of what death is and its confining characteristics. But we are free; as the Christ said," death where is your victory where is your sting."

FREE WILL

The subject of free will has been hinted at to some degree during this discourse. Many people in a democratic society claim to have free will. They believe they are free to come and go as they please and say what is on their hearts and minds. However even within that environment you may not be free to express an un-democratic view point. So it may be that free will as we see it is merely a set of allowed expressions. Some seems more open then others but all of them having a limit to that expression. Hence we all experience a limit in our expression. Therefore we are not really free. To compound the matter every expression is in some way bolstered by an influence. The way we think, speak, dress, and form opinions is a direct reflection of the localized influences we experience. So while we think we are having an original idea we are really a continuation of many influences. One idea stacked upon another. There has not been a free human being since the dawn of man. We have been and are slaves. All mankind is caught in slavery so pervasive he cannot witness it. He is given allowances so that he thinks he's free. But if you attempt to stray from the designated path magically some hardship will fall upon you. Some wondered how mankind developed the concept of slavery. The pristine life form could not have seen such an event in its infancy. In its original environs there were no influences. Once influences came into play and the pristine life form was awakened (or became self aware) it witnessed the power of influences and slavery was born. We now practice slavery as a matter of existence because we are slaves. It could be argued that a lack of self-awareness will destroy slavery at its root freeing mankind. However at this time we live in environs loaded with influences from which we cannot extricate ourselves. Witness the path of destruction we are on that we cannot extricate ourselves from. We see the direction we are headed but we cannot stop ourselves from going in that direction. We have become slaves to fear and other influences. When messengers come they usually exhibit the ability to walk without influence. This is the Great power. Then the world will raise the level of influence to convince them to stray.

But that great light shines when the messenger does not yield. Sometimes death is the ultimate influence. We have all seen this. So to summarize there is no such event as free will in the life force called mankind. He is embroidered in a matrix of slavery so deep he does not see it. The only way the life force can have free will is for it to first not be self-aware and second exist in environs without influences. Since we have neither there is no free will.

SONS OF SLAVERY

This is a somewhat personal dictation to the Sons of slavery, those whose offspring were the remnants of slaves. We have the distinction of being a remnant that God chose to remain as close to the original designation of mankind as possible. He allowed our suffering so that we could not be caught up in the headlong march toward self destruction. This may seem like a contradiction of realities but rest assured that this is a fact. Mankind in its thirst to attain God-like knowledge and understanding has lost its basic foundation. That foundation is LOVE. Though we may seem to be behind in technological successes we retain the basic element of life. Now the world seeks our destruction for it knows that we cannot be converted in our entirety. We remain the hope of life in this world. We have not been abandoned as it may seem but persevered for that great moment when God shall show his strength in a people discarded by the world but preserved to God Almighty. We are now awakened to that calling. Do not despair. God has prevailed.

THE BIG PICTURE

So now we attempt to show the big picture. The small picture is mankind proper. At mankind proper we see a life engrossed in itself and aware of itself alone. It does not know that it is part of a larger life form called earth and it is supremely not aware of the life form called the universe and it is ultimately not aware of the life force called Almighty God. We study the earth as though it is not alive we study the universe as though it is a machine. We are alive physically so the universe must be alive. The life of the universe must come from life again. There is only one Life in all existence. That life is one. No one has a life of his own. All life belongs to God and God is one. So the sensation called my life is error or better stated a fabrication. If you have your own life you will lose it if you lose your life you will gain it in the oneness. In the oneness there would be no error or such events as murder for to do so would be to destroy ones own. War would and could not exist. Hatred would and could not exist. All the darkness that exist in mankind could not exist. It would all fail. Scientist are bewildered by a force they called dark energy. It is a force that seems to be pushing apart the universe. Perhaps they are witnessing the growing energy of a life form from within. Calculations will not all you to see life growing. Life will never fit in a calculation. To know that we are a small but love component in an eternal life form is a humbling experience. But Paul the apostle said it best in HIM (God) "we live and move and have our being".

VIRUS

S in exists as a spiritual virus. It was inserted to the soul via the respondent. It appears to enter at action which is probably why mankind has failed to conquer it. We believe that our actions are sin when they are actually the results of sin. By the time the action has occurred sin is well established. We shall begin to show the insertion and how, when and where it occurred. At The fall of man the virus is hidden at the question, "Has God indeed said, "You shall not eat of every tree of the garden"? This seemingly harmless question was asked to gain access to the life form. It served as a sort of break—in program needed to steal access to the operating systems of the life form. Like a computer, in order for the virus to take affect you must respond. As soon as the woman responds the virus has gained access. When the woman gives her response of what God has instructed her she is now unwittingly a carrier. After that the woman, who has seen the Forbidden tree before, now sees it as desirable for food. Before the question she did not have this desire. When she saw the tree as desirable you see that the virus is working to rewrite the life form from" All" to conscious "I". Then suddenly they became self aware they began too see the world as singular and separated life forms. The virus was working. They found themselves aware of themselves only (their eyes were opened). The virus has taken. When God came looking for them they were not accessible. They were not invisible to God for we know that God sees everything. They were however rerouted in another system controlled by the serpent. So you hear God say something that never should be said "where are you"? This question is singularly the most disturbing one of all. Now they were in a totally different system of which we remain to this day. There is however now an exit, that exit is the very essence of God called the Son of God. So we understand that it is at respondent where we fail. The law does not address respondent. You simply have to respond so that access is granted to the adversary. This intrusion was so subtle they never saw it coming. We today never see it coming. If you think of it most opportunity to fail happens in the heart before any actions take place. We respond then fail. We don't fail then respond. If you are dead to something you will not respond no matter what. However if you become alive to something it is a good chance you will be a respondent to it. The law addresses action not respondent. The law seeks to control the effects of sin not its root cause. The example that was previously given was the common cold. Our cold remedies address the symptoms not the rhino virus which is the cause. To recognize the sin virus and how it is spiritually contracted is tantamount to its cure. It is really imperative that the cultural understanding of the gospel is not one of religious intent but one of understanding. Religion profits nothing. Mankind cannot cure himself. Religion seems to imply that mankind has the capabilities to self-correct. Have we been able to put the proverbial egg back together? There is no evidence to the affirmative.

There is a problem with this understanding the Christ (in his confrontation with the devil) seems to be a respondent when he is questioned. If he was respondent why didn't he fail like the first Adam? Although he seems to be respondent the virus does not take. When he responds it is not a self-inspired response this seems to be the only difference in the two confrontations. The first Adam responds for self-preservation the second does not. So it appears that it is not just responding that allows the invasion of sin it must be a self-preserving or self-gratifying response that allows the virus to invade. If we don't respond selfishly the virus is rejected. In order to not respond selfishly the old nature must die. We will otherwise be carriers of this vile disease and will unwittingly deliver it to generations to come.

HELL

This is another misunderstood concept in the teachings of God. The concept of hell is that, all that is not deemed worthy by God is descended into hell and eventually the lake of fire. Fire is used either to burn/destroy or purify something. Since the opportunity to purify is in God it is probably safe to say that hell is not for purification but destruction. The problem with the understanding of hell is the premise of personal existence. Since God is all there are **no personal existences.** Sin is the sensation of a personal existence.

Since this sensation is a fabrication or lie it is not real. Those fabrications are the only things that God wants to destroy and by doing so he purifies all life. Those fabrications are reserved in hell and destroyed in the lake of fire. So in reality nothing" real" goes to hell or burns in the lake of fire, only fabrications and variants of the illusion called a personal existence. So some would say why would a loving God send someone to hell? Well they would be correct; he doesn't, He simply disposes of that which is not real. That which is in hell is not real. We have to remember that Adam died at personal existence i.e. "who told you that you were naked" Adam became self-aware which is a lie. So God does not destroy life in hell and the lake of fire. He destroys lies and illusions called personal existence. So you could be a good person and still burn in the fire. There are Good and evil angels and they too will burn in the fire. Only the express image of God shall remain and in him is no sensation called "I". So if "I" dies in us (which is the example of the cross) there should be no concern for an encounter with hell or the lake of fire. We have to surrender these lives back to the owner. The lives were never ours. This is perhaps the most difficult faith item. We feel as though we have been in possession of the existence all the while. We have the sensation that to give up the life means not doing this or that. The giving up of life means the sensation of the One Life has arrived and the old sensation is gone. The sensation called my life is gone. It is not something that can occur by effort. This is a spiritual journey. So to return to the One Life is the original state of the life form. We never ever had a life. This whole sensation called personal existence is a lie. When you were first born you did not have this sensation. We had no personal sensation and were without shame, when you become self-aware sin has arrived. We unwittingly spread sin to our offspring just by the nature of our being. Sin feels absolutely real the life that we seem to hold seems real but all of this is a lie. Those lies will find themselves deposited in the lake of fire. Real life is quite remarkable and beyond comprehension and unspeakable. God has never assigned real life to hell or the lake of fire. The day we become self-aware is the day we start our life in the illusion. May we all die well.

THE UNSEEN

Assuming the reader has made it this far and has not lost focus we shall speak of the unseen. As stated before we cannot be seen. To even speak of this is bordering on the place of no return. There is a certain preciseness that must be used. We cannot be seen or differentiated as individuals. All deeds done by the life form are without recognition. If there was a witness the witness would recognize that the deeds were of value to life. These deeds however should be of no more consequence than someone taking a breath or a bee pollinating a flower. To be seen is death and destruction. To call oneself good or evil is tantamount to destruction. If we recall again the words of the Most High when all creation was made "it was good". All action performed after that has to be of the Creator and cannot be witnessed. It is written that he who bears witness of himself his witness is false. Mankind however has his eyes opened and as the Christ said because you say "I see" your sins remain with you. Perhaps now we may come to understand how truly far we are from the Creator. If we are successful we will again be amongst the unseen for all eternity. Seems strange but in the end we shall be seen no more. There will be no notion of origin or being seen which is the domain of the dead. This isn't going to be easy the world is very enticing there are more than enough temptations to a being that exist in the "seen" arena. If we however did not exist there none of these would even be an issue. The battleground is set but we are more than conquerors. All things are possible to those who believe.

THE DOOR

The "Door" is actually a reference to the conquerors reward. So we begin with a little history. First we wish to distinguish that creation is subject to God or better said God created existence. The physical natures and spiritual nature of heaven and earth are part of creation. God however is above existence for when he spoke existence came into being. In the bible the first thing God accomplished was to make existence. God is therefore above all with creation being his throne. Lucifer was the first creature in all creation and he covered all of creation. Lucifer was there when creation was just a smoldering furnace of materials. God said he was with him at the stones of fire. He covered all of creation and was its glory and was called" the anointed cherub who covers". Because of the multitude of things that were in creation(as God said" by the multitude of his merchandise) and the beauty of those things Lucifer sinned and was expelled from heaven. We must remember this is all in creation as God is above creation. Lucifer had no place until Adam surrendered this provincial to him. Now the devil(as Lucifer is now called) seeks to transform this life form to his image. He now seeks to deceive mankind into a self contained nature. Once mankind goes to a self contained existence he makes himself subject to creation in the stimulus response environment, where mankind is immediately enslaved. The spiritual nature of man has to have a nature that is above creation. A natural man will use intellect in a beastly fashion. The nature of man must be the nature of God, mankind will otherwise destroy himself. All the intellect in the universe cannot save humanity for these vessels are the compatible with the spirit of God alone. We have one hope, to be born again. Which leads us to the Door. All explanations end at the Door.

THE HOLY SPIRIT

Wow! A simple expression of amazement but perfect for this understanding. Speaking of the Holy Spirit is like your life force or the coldest glass of water on a hot day. To see a human being is nothing without the Holy Spirit. If the dust of the earth was no more the Holy Spirit would abound. All life force is the Holy Spirit. IT is the Holy Spirit which sustains the physical nature of all creation. The Holy spirit is God's nature and is one with the Son of God those three are one. The nature of mankind does not permit this understanding. Mankind is forever trapped in the conscious "I" awareness. It is as if the person who said the earth is not flat, because we can't see beyond our horizons we won't be able to comprehend. The Holy Spirit is God. When you first meet the Holy Spirit you won't be able to comprehend the Holy Spirit. The Holy Spirit will teach you and guild you along your way until the day that you and the Holy Spirit become one. On that day you will be one with The Father, Son and the Holy Spirit. As was said before Wow!

PERFECTION

Most of us would like to wish that we were perfect, we would have no critics or complainers. We work everyday toward an ideal which we consider is as close to perfect as we envision. One interesting visual is that perfection alone is deadly. We must recall that Lucifer was perfect in wisdom and beauty then vanity destroyed him. Perhaps the perfection alone killed him (spiritually). We submit that perfection without humility is a death sentence. Humility does not appear to be a created essence. Paul was given a "thorn in the flesh" to bring humility to his soaring popularity. Humility protects us from perfection. When we become closer to God our humility will increase, our mere consciousness will be insufficient to cope. You would not want perfection without humility.

www.ingramcontent.com/pod-product-compliance
Lightning Source LLC
Chambersburg PA
CBHW021252280526
45784CB00005B/2347